After

Timberlake Wertenbaker's plays include *New Anatomies* (ICA, London, 1982), *Abel's Sister* (Royal Court, Theatre Upstairs, London, 1984), *The Grace of Mary Traverse* (Royal Court, main stage, London), which won the Plays and Players Most Promising Playwright Award 1985, *Our Country's Good* (Royal Court, main stage, London and Broadway), winner of the Laurence Olivier Play of the Year Award in 1988 and New York Drama Critics' Circle Award for Best New Foreign Play in 1991, *The Love of the Nightingale* (Royal Shakespeare Company's Other Place, Stratford-upon-Avon), which won the 1989 Eileen Anderson Central TV Drama Award, *Three Birds Alighting on a Field* (Royal Court, main stage, London), which won the Susan Smith Blackburn Award, Writers' Guild Award and London Critics' Circle Award in 1992, *The Break of Day* (Out of Joint Production, Royal Court, London, and touring, 1995) and *After Darwin* (Hampstead Theatre, London, 1998). She has written the screenplay of *The Children*, based on Edith Wharton's novel, and a BBC2 film entitled *Do Not Disturb*. Translations include Marivaux's *False Admissions* and *Successful Strategies* for Shared Experience, Marivaux's *La Dispute*, Jean Anouilh's *Leocadia*, Maurice Maeterlinck's *Pelleas and Melisande* for BBC Radio, Ariane Mnouchkine's *Mephisto*, adapted for the RSC in 1986, Sophocles' *The Theban Plays* (RSC, London and Stratford, 1991) and Euripides' *Hecuba* (San Francisco, 1995).

TIMBERLAKE WERTENBAKER

After Darwin

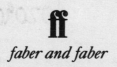

faber and faber

For J.

First published in 1998
by Faber and Faber Limited
3 Queen Square London WC1N 3AU

Typeset by Faber and Faber Ltd
Printed in England by Mackays of Chatham plc, Chatham, Kent

© Timberlake Wertenbaker, 1998

Timberlake Wertenbaker is hereby identified as author of this
work in accordance with Section 77 of the Copyright,
Designs and Patents Act 1988

All rights in this play are strictly reserved and applications for any use what-
soever, including performance rights, must be made in advance, prior to any
such proposed use, to Casarotto Ramsay Ltd., National House, 60–66
Wardour Street, London W1V 3HP

A CIP record for this book
is available from the British Library

ISBN 0–571–19584–9

2 4 6 8 10 9 7 5 3 1

Characters

Robert FitzRoy
Charles Darwin
Millie
Ian
Tom
Lawrence

After Darwin was first performed at Hampstead Theatre, London, on 8 July 1998 with the following cast:

Charles Darwin/Tom Jason Watkins
Robert FitzRoy/Ian Michael Feast
Millie Ingeborga Dapkunaite
Lawrence Colin Salmon

Director Lindsay Posner
Set Designer Joanna Parker
Lighting Designer Peter Mumford
Sound John A. Leonard
Assistant Director Adam Rush

Note: This text preceded the first production. Changes may have been made in rehearsal.

Act One

SCENE ONE: 'DESPAIR'

30 April 1865. 7 a.m.
A room that is elegant and spare. On a large table, a washing bowl, a cut-throat razor.
Robert FitzRoy wears full navy uniform minus the jacket, which hangs. Charles Darwin, in rumpled clothes, sits on a chair to the side.
FitzRoy holds a Bible in his hand and brandishes it.

FitzRoy This is the truth. 'Woe unto thee, blind guide . . .' Natural selection? We cannot survive without The Book. You want a grim future, without purpose, mockery of all that is sacred, no moral light. 'It had been better for that man if he had not been born.' I harboured you in my cabin. I, FitzRoy of *The Beagle*, have brought destruction on the world – 'Woe unto that man by whom the offence cometh.' That nose, that nose, why did I tear up the letter? (*Pause.*) I only ever wanted to do what was right. I understood it, it was my inheritance – but perhaps there is no right, no good. Forgive me, God, for what I have done, for what I am about to do – if you are there.

He brandishes the razor at Darwin, who does not react.

You were the mediocrity, I had the destiny – you scrambled my destiny, and the world. (*He turns away.*) Perhaps God never looked. The fittest, so-called, grimacing their success. Thousands like you in this world sodden with vulgarity. No more like me. They laugh at me. No more now. I leave nothing behind. (*to Darwin*) But you never saw the pain of extinction. (*He draws the razor up to his throat to slit it.*)

SCENE TWO: 'HOPE'

4 September 1831.
  The Beagle.
  Captain Robert FitzRoy in full navy uniform, dazzling. Charles Darwin in rumpled travelling clothes.
  The presence of wealth and elegance, very spare and neat. Chronometers.

FitzRoy Tenerife, the Cape de Verde Islands, Rio de Janeiro, the Straits of Magellan, the Falkland Islands, the Galapagos Islands, do these names mean anything to you, Mr Darwin?

Darwin I've read about Tenerife, Captain FitzRoy, I've dreamt of Rio.

FitzRoy We do not know the exact longitude of Rio. If *The Beagle* can chart these waters and coasts accurately, she will change the history of the world. I have twenty-two chronometers on board.

Darwin Twenty-two!

FitzRoy The Admiralty provided four, I bought the rest. No more shipwrecks, think of the lives saved . . .

Darwin Yes!

FitzRoy And then the souls . . . In Tierra del Fuego I encountered the most miserable and savage creatures. I captured four and had them educated in England.

Darwin Indeed, Captain FitzRoy . . . I heard of York Minster, Jemmy Button and Fuegia – euh –

FitzRoy Basket. The fourth, Boat Memory, died of the small pox. I am particularly pleased with Jemmy Button, who seems naturally disposed to civilization – I am bringing all three back with a young missionary who will establish a settlement on that wild coast. I have an artist on board to record the flora, fauna, most remarkable in these parts.

Darwin Yes.

FitzRoy There lacks only a gentleman savant.

Darwin Yes!

FitzRoy To pursue researches in natural history, collecting, observing, noting . . . A companion as well: the coast of South America is bleak. The previous captain of *The Beagle* shot himself, you heard?

Darwin No, I deeply regret –

FitzRoy When I took command of the ship, the crew were near mutiny . . . (*Pause. He studies Darwin.*) Mr Darwin, I regret I was not able to get a message to you in time, but the post of naturalist on *The Beagle* has already been filled . . .

Darwin Ah! Oh, no . . .

FitzRoy I have only now written the letter confirming my decision. I hope you are not too disappointed?

Darwin Bitterly! Forgive me, Captain, if it is too late, I must now . . . I won't take any more of your time. Ah! . . .

FitzRoy I was not under the impression you were so keen.

Darwin I came as soon as I could! (*Pause.*) My father opposed the idea. I could do nothing without his approval.

FitzRoy He fears for your safety?

Darwin He thinks I'm wayward.

FitzRoy So.

Darwin But Uncle Jos – that's my uncle Josiah Wedgwood – thought it would be a capital thing to do and convinced my father. My father wants me to take Holy Orders, but the pursuit of Natural History is very suitable to a clergyman and it would only be a delay . . . We answered all of his objections and my father agreed.

FitzRoy Your father is an excellent doctor. He once treated an aunt of mine and she lived until she was ninety-five.

Darwin He is most shrewd, yes – that is, he used to take me on his rounds, he wanted me to follow him into medicine.

FitzRoy And you did not feel compelled to obey his wishes?

Darwin I hate the sight of blood.

FitzRoy I could not have guaranteed your safety in South America, Mr Darwin.

Darwin It's not my own blood I'm afraid of spilling, Captain FitzRoy, it's dissection. I shoot accurately, I assure you. I'm not very good at taxidermy though – and the lectures were so tedious! My father fears I have no application . . . (*He stops himself.*)

FitzRoy You have eminent friends at Cambridge.

Darwin I'm frightfully clever at catching beetles, Captain. Perhaps it's just as well for the Coleoptera of South America I'm not coming.

FitzRoy Professor John Henslow – his father was master of the royal dockyards at Chatham –

Darwin He's taught me everything I know about Botany –

FitzRoy Adam Sedgwick – they say his geology lectures are always full . . . What made you so wish to come?

Darwin Alexander von Humboldt.

FitzRoy You've read him?

Darwin Everything. You too?

FitzRoy At naval college: (*recites*) 'From my earliest youth I felt an ardent desire to travel into distant regions seldom visited by Europeans –'. So did I.

Darwin It was Humboldt's description of Tenerife that first made me –

FitzRoy Yes! Climbing that volcano.

Darwin And then the Orinoco . . .

FitzRoy I lived on that canoe. We shall be far south of Humboldt's Venezuela, but there are great rivers in Brazil, Mr Darwin – (*Pause*.) And do you admire Jane Austen?

Darwin I have not read her — yet.

FitzRoy I have all of her books on board.

Darwin I did read Coldstream and Foggo when I heard I might come on this voyage, I studied astronomy – I believe I can follow calculations for longitude and latitude, I even plunged into fearful descriptions of storms at sea . . .

FitzRoy I have fitted *The Beagle* with a lightning conductor, making her the safest vessel in the navy. The perils of ship life are more internal, Mr Darwin: bad temper in the sailors, melancholy in ourselves . . . the soul of a man may seem to die. You seem to have a cheerful temperament. It must make you a pleasant companion. Your family are Whigs, are they not?

Darwin Especially the Wedgwoods.

FitzRoy The FitzRoys have always been Tories. We are opposing your reforms, Mr Darwin, this dangerous tide of liberalism . . .

Darwin I find beetles and rocks occupy my thoughts. I am singularly ignorant of politics.

FitzRoy That is because you are still young.

Darwin You are only two years older than I, Captain FitzRoy.

FitzRoy One grows fast in the navy. I went to sea at fourteen.

Darwin I lost my mother when I was seven and was perhaps spoiled by my sisters. I kept running away from school to be back with them.

FitzRoy My mother died when I was five. (*Embarrassed pause.*) I did invite a friend of mine on board, Mr Darwin – I want a companion as much as a man of science, you understand – but he refused this morning. This letter is to another friend, a Tory – but he hasn't read Humboldt. (*He tears up the letter.*) I shall write to the Admiralty and ask them to agree to your joining *The Beagle*.

Darwin Captain! I am – overcome! *Gloria in excelsis*. Beetles of South America, here I come! Forgive me . . .

FitzRoy You may find your spirits constrained by the lack of space, but I shall do all in my power to make you comfortable. Come to the ship tomorrow. You'll need a good pair of pistols, I shall help you choose them, books, although you'll find my library extensive, I'll give you a list of clothes –

Darwin I shall follow your guidance in all matters . . . I have never been at sea before!

FitzRoy stiffens and studies Darwin for a moment.

FitzRoy Mr Darwin, forgive me for the apparent impertinence of my question, but does your father have your nose?

Darwin I believe he does . . . Mine is somewhat smaller . . .

FitzRoy According to the laws of physiognomy, it indicates a certain weakness of temperament. Nothing I hear about your father confirms this.

Darwin No, my father is not weak. (*Pause.*) I've always hated my nose.

FitzRoy No matter. I have great faith in your friends and I myself am no mean judge of character. I shall be delighted to have you on *The Beagle* and you shall help me fulfil another purpose. William Buckland, as you know, has found conclusive evidence of the Flood in England.

Darwin Not quite conclusive –

FitzRoy We could establish such a proof in South America. Your mentor Henslow is a deeply religious man, I understand.

Darwin He once told me he would not want a single word of the Thirty-nine Articles changed.

FitzRoy Do we not live in a great age? Our natural philosophers trace God's signature on Earth as our English ships mark the contours of the world. I shall prevent shipwrecks by mapping the coasts, but together, Mr Darwin, we shall prevent spiritual shipwreck by mapping God's work.

Darwin I shall do all I can to be of help, Captain FitzRoy.

The present.
  Millie, Tom (Darwin) and Ian (FitzRoy).

Millie Embrace!

  Nobody moves.

Embrace: hug tight. You are both so happy, so full of hope and love for each other, you embrace.

Ian Englishmen don't embrace, Millie, particularly not these Englishmen.

Millie I don't mean homosexual, I mean emotion.

Ian Emotion –

Millie This great, this beautiful emotion of friendship, it's so obvious you embrace, isn't it, Tom?

Tom It's just that – you see – we – I mean, they – may have trouble expressing – you know: English, all that – maybe we could just move towards each other –

Millie Charles Darwin is young, enthusiastic, surely you want to embrace your beau ideal of a captain.

Tom Whatever.

Ian I have read everything there is about FitzRoy, which isn't much, I admit, but I can assure you he would not embrace or be embraced – he would never show what he feels.

Millie Ian, you are creating him.

Ian He is an historical character, I am finding him.

Millie You say yourself he is unknown. He will evolve into what we make him here.

Ian Why make him a fool? The phrenology business is bad enough, can't we get rid of it?

Millie It's a famous anecdote.

Ian I don't like it.

Millie You don't like anything.

Tom Ian likes the lines, Millie, he gets so angry when I get them wrong.

Millie I see emotion in these lines.

Ian You interpret.

Millie I see two men who embrace.

Ian Maybe in Bulgaria.

Millie In Bulgaria, they would take a knife to their arms and mingle their blood. And they would not be young men on an exciting voyage around the world, they would be fighting in caves and forests against the Turks. And perhaps one would betray the other, so there would be fear and also anger against the oppressor and perhaps both would be tortured, mangled – dead!

Ian And now that you've once again shamed us with the excitement of your history you expect us to do as you want?

Millie It is not my history any more, this is my history.

Ian Then you should learn to understand repression. It may not be as romantic as oppression but it works.

Millie I do not want some gloomy English Chekhov here, Ian, I want light and tenderness. It is thought tenderness gave mammals an evolutionary advantage.

Tom It did? I have tenderness – I think.

Ian It is 1831. I am a captain in His Majesty's Navy, I am an aristocrat and I am English, I am not playing an evolving mammal!

Millie FitzRoy is religious, he knows tenderness.

Ian Not in the Church of England.

Millie I do not see how we go on. (She *throws herself down at Ian's feet.*) I beg you, I entreat you, I supplicate, I fall on my knees before you – to express emotion.

Ian This is no way to direct.

Millie It is in Moscow.

Tom I like this tenderness thing. Ian, we can try a little tenderness, can't we, repressed even, yeah?

SCENE FOUR: 'TENDERNESS'

January 1832.
The Bay of Biscay. FitzRoy's cabin. A storm. The ship rolls.
Darwin stands, sways, very seasick.
FitzRoy arranges a hammock.

FitzRoy Try this, Darwin, it may help.

Darwin tries to get into the hammock. He has trouble. FitzRoy holds it for him. Darwin reels.

You must believe me when I say this is the worst storm I have encountered in the Bay of Biscay.

Darwin I fear I shall prove useless on this voyage.

FitzRoy We have not been at sea very long.

Darwin I was sick as soon as we left the Channel. Even the Fuegians laugh at me. Have you seen Jemmy Button mimicking my sickness?

FitzRoy He doesn't mean it unkindly. They're better mimics than our London actors.

Darwin holds down a retch.

Perhaps if you lay down on my divan.

FitzRoy gently leads Darwin to the divan. Darwin collapses.

Darwin This is intolerable.

FitzRoy Lieutenant Wickham tells me you are considering leaving *The Beagle*.

Darwin I cannot be much of a companion in this state, Captain, I might stay in Tenerife and then find a ship to take me home.

FitzRoy I heard in Portsmouth there is a quarantine in Tenerife. We may have to remain aboard.

Darwin I had so hoped to see it!

FitzRoy I am sorry to disappoint you, Darwin, but you will find much to see in the Cape de Verde Islands. My officers would be sorry to see their dear Philosopher go. You have made yourself well liked. I should be sorry, too. Very sorry.

Darwin wrestles with a bout of seasickness. FitzRoy gently adjusts a pillow.

Let me read you the next chapter of *Persuasion*.

SCENE FIVE: 'FRIENDSHIP'

Tom and Ian, as before, but very relaxed.

Tom I really admire you, I saw you a few years ago. Yeah, I thought, yeah. I hope I'm not letting you down.

Ian Not at all.

Tom It's a lot of lines.

Ian You'll get them.

Tom I remember them, I just don't know what they mean – and then, words . . . They shift about.

Ian That's the pleasure.

Tom In a film, you're there for ever. Fixed.

Ian And people eat popcorn while they watch.

Tom I went to read for this film.

Ian When?

Tom I know, I'm not supposed to. They're looking for Germans, I mean, English with German accents, real Germans are too expensive or too real or something. What do you think?

Ian About Germans?

Tom Would you do a film?

Ian I'm not asked. Listen, we have a lot of words coming up.

Tom Yeah, sure, words. Will you help me? You know, hints.

Ian Concentrate.

Tom Concentrate.

Ian You don't really need my help.

Tom I know, but I like it.

SCENE SIX: 'DOUBT'

Darwin and FitzRoy.
A month later, off the coast of South America.
It is hot. Darwin reads with enthusiasm.

Darwin '– The next morning we saw the sun rise behind the outline of the Grand Canary island and suddenly illumine the peak of Tenerife, whilst the lower parts were veiled in fleecy clouds.'

FitzRoy Fleecy?

Darwin 'On the sixteenth of January we anchored at Porto Praya.'

FitzRoy You've gone from Devonport to the Cape de Verde Islands in one paragraph?

Darwin I was rather seasick.

FitzRoy Go on.

Darwin 'February twenty-ninth: the day has passed delightfully. Delight itself, however, is a weak term to express the feelings –'

FitzRoy Feelings.

Darwin '– feelings of a naturalist who, for the first time, has wandered by himself in a Brazilian forest. The elegance of the grasses –'

FitzRoy Elegance? Is that a size?

Darwin 'The novelty of the parasitical plants, the beauty of the flowers –'

FitzRoy Vague, Darwin, vague . . .

Darwin 'The glossy green of the foliage – A most paradoxical mixture of sound and silence pervades the shady parts of the wood.'

FitzRoy Which is it?

Darwin I explain the noise from the insects is loud but there is a deep silence in the forest. 'To a person fond of natural history, such a day as this brings with it a deeper pleasure than he can ever hope to experience again!'

FitzRoy Such enthusiasm. So few facts. (*Pause.*) Of course, you don't have to publish it.

Darwin No.

FitzRoy And so much of your personality. Think of Humboldt, those scientific descriptions.

Darwin It was his enthusiasm that infected me. I believed it did you.

FitzRoy Each night, Darwin, I sit here for hours and write up everything I have observed and done during the day. I had better give you my own description of our departure. (*He reads, fast, but with pride.*) 'Vessels in the offing, and distant land looming much; a few mottled, hard-edged clouds appearing in the east; streaks (mare's tails across the sky) spreading from the same quarter; a high barometer (30.3) and the smoke of chimneys rising high into the air and going westwards, were the signs which assured us of a favourable wind.' (*Brief pause.*) I've taken a whole chapter to discuss the purpose of the voyage, the Fuegians and my civilizing mission, the refitting of the ship, I explain we are seventy-four on board, even you are mentioned by name, Darwin, and it is not until the end of the third chapter that I reach the Cape de Verde Islands – having discussed the possible causes of the high waves in the Atlantic, how to foresee a squall, problems of determining longitude. Nothing is omitted from my account of the Voyage of *The*

Beagle – I know how interested people will be in reading it. Observe and note down. Observe again. Never trust memory. I suggest you tear up your account and start again.

Darwin folds up his papers and puts them in his pocket. A pause.

Perhaps I expect too much of people.

Darwin You do not spare yourself.

FitzRoy We strive for perfection and so mirror God.

Darwin God taught forgiveness.

FitzRoy You still reproach me for the floggings?

Darwin Thirty-five lashes for a little drunkenness the day after Christmas.

FitzRoy I go on at great length about the necessity of flogging in these chapters.

Darwin I shall read them with interest.

FitzRoy Are you doubting me?

Darwin doesn't answer.

From the ship's crew I expect only obedience, but I would wish for you to understand me. When we round Cape Horn we will face storms, winds, rocks – the most dismal and dank surroundings. A captain who cannot assert discipline betrays his men, goes mad himself, mad . . . the word discipline means little to you.

Darwin I've encountered so little of it in nature.

FitzRoy Darwin, we sail into Rio tomorrow and I shall make sure we arrive at dawn as I did the first time I saw it. It is the most beautiful harbour in the world and will lift our spirits. And you can take time away from the ship to explore the interior.

Darwin Thank you, Captain FitzRoy.

FitzRoy You see I am not without sensibility – but there is so much at stake.

Darwin You work yourself very hard.

FitzRoy Too hard? Who is saying that? Wickham, Sulivan? They call me Black Coffee, don't they – when the dark mood descends –

Darwin Your lieutenants are devoted to you, Captain FitzRoy. I have only observed.

SCENE SEVEN: 'CAMOUFLAGE'

Tom and Ian, pacing around each other.

Ian No. No. No. In his autobiography, he describes himself as a simpleton who only accidentally stumbled on one of those theories that change the world. He was a good and faithful husband, adored by his children, a sound friend, brother – haven't you read anything?

Tom Millie brought me some books, I looked at the pictures. All I'm saying is, he's not nice. Nobody can be nice and that famous. You're nice, but you're not famous, I mean, you're in *Who's Who*, but you're not – like – you're not a film star.

Ian You're playing a superstar of history, Mr Millennium man himself, you ought to work harder. He did.

Tom You want to play him . . .

Ian Everybody loves the winner, especially if he's decent.

Tom Darwin wasn't nice just now and he's horrible to FitzRoy later.

Ian Something happened on that ship, Darwin seemed to need to obliterate FitzRoy's memory.

Tom You see, not nice. It's the struggle whatchamacall it. For Darwin to go up, FitzRoy has to be pulverized. (*He makes a grinding sound.*)

Ian You can be honourable and survive.

Tom Yeah –? Before I became an actor I thought of being a soldier. You know why?

Ian It requires even less intellectual effort.

Tom Because I loved the idea of camouflage. It's a great survival tactic, you even win wars that way. Listen, it goes this way: there's this great idea, the struggle for survival.

Ian Existence. Get that right!

Tom Yeah, whatever. How was this idea going to survive in a world of FitzRoys? You use camouflage. Maybe even the idea uses camouflage, uses Darwin the nice – but not so nice – you see – in fact, ruthless –

Ian Don't tell Millie that, she's so in love with him and with you.

Tom That's because I'm nice to her. FitzRoy never learned.

Ian I can't stand all that emotion.

Tom Emotion's very fashionable now.

Ian Real passion comes from ideas.

Tom Yeah. That's why I wanted to do this, I wanted to look intelligent, for an experience, you know. But I'm in a muddle with this guy. He's like one of his fossils in the next scene: put the bits this way you get a giant snake, that way, a furry mammoth – you're supposed to help me – you're so experienced – so nice.

Ian I've told you: read the books.

Tom Why should I believe the books?

Ian It's called history.

Tom Yeah, but history's shifty too, I mean, isn't it supposed to be rewritten all the time? Things happened that we were told never happened, like those Yugoslavs who helped us in the war – you know – the partisans those English politicians sent back to be killed – it's in the film script. And then some things that maybe didn't happen, like the Holocaust.

Ian moves to seize Tom, quick and violent.

Ian Don't you ever say that, ever!

Tom OK, sorry. Don't get so emotional.

Ian Even your stupidity doesn't excuse a statement like that.

Tom I'm only repeating what I hear. I don't care one way or the other. (*He begins to lug bags into the middle of the cabin.*)

Ian Don't you?

Tom I wasn't there. Were you?

Ian We all carry the luggage.

Tom Not me. I live in the present. I travel light.

SCENE EIGHT: 'CHANGE'

Montevideo.
  FitzRoy's cabin.
  Darwin lugs some dusty bags. He is himself dusty, dishevelled. The cabin is filled with dust.

18

FitzRoy sits, very still, very dark.

Darwin I rode with the Gauchos. They are so tall, handsome, proud, dissolute: long hair, black moustaches, clicking spurs and knives. So polite. (*He imitates a Spanish accent, rather badly.*) 'Si, Signor Darwin . . . ' but offend their dignity and – (*He imitates the slitting of a throat.*) I watched them catch their cattle with the *lazo*. Like this. (*He twirls an imaginary lasso.*) I tried it myself, but I tangled my own horse's legs and we both fell. How they laughed. Said they'd never seen a man capture his own self before. Ha. Ha. Ha. There was I, and the horse, both wrapped in the *lazo* like a naturalist's parcel –

He falls on the ground to demonstrate. FitzRoy offers a wintry smile.

We climbed the Sierra de las Animas. I found eighty different sorts of birds. I'll show you. All kinds of reptiles, even a ninety-eight pound water hog! The buck I shot had the worst smell I've ever encountered. I used my handkerchief on him, I think I can still smell it.

FitzRoy So can I.

Darwin We came to a salt lake of black mud, fetid. Ugh. I brought some mud back for you but I dropped the bottle. I'm sorry.

FitzRoy There seems to be some mud still stuck on your coat.

Darwin There were hundreds of flamingoes. The life, FitzRoy – on this seemingly grim and barren landscape. The flamingoes feed on worms, the worms on infusoria or confervae, all the life is totally adapted to this lake of brine, isn't it wonderful?

FitzRoy God's infinite providence.

Darwin Here's the best. (*He takes out some large and dusty fossilized bones with great care.*) I have many more coming. Wickham will be so cross with me. He can't find any more room on the ship!

FitzRoy raises his eyebrows at this. Darwin places the bones on the floor as well as some teeth and a skull. It is all very heavy.

Some of these crumble as you touch them, it's maddening.

FitzRoy Quite.

Darwin This animal was as large as a rhinoceros. The tooth could have belonged to an elephant. It's the tooth of a herbivore. And look at this: a neck like a giraffe's. (*He keeps placing and replacing bones, puzzling over the configuration.*) These animals are no longer found in South America. What happened?

FitzRoy The door of the Ark may not have been large enough to accommodate them.

Darwin Ha! Ha! Ha!

FitzRoy May I ask what amuses you so?

Darwin Surely, FitzRoy – Aren't you reading Lyell's second volume?

FitzRoy I run a ship!

Darwin Surely you agree with him that you can't explain all you find on high mountains by a catastrophic flood, but rather by a very slow – why, you said yourself –

FitzRoy I hadn't considered the consequences of such a statement. And Lyell fudges.

Darwin He proposes –

FitzRoy Waffle! Something must be one thing or another.

There was a flood: the Bible tells us so.

A short silence. Darwin goes to another sack and brings out a dead mole-like creature.

Darwin They call it the tuco-tuco, because of the sound it makes. (*He makes the sound: 'tuco tuco'.*) They're very friendly. (*He brings out a dead starling.*) A kind of starling. They stand on the backs of cows and horses. Listen. (*He imitates a bird sound with a bubbly hiss.*) It seems they deposit their eggs in other nests like our cuckoos. Now listen to this. (*He emits a high-pitched sound like a peewit.*) Just like a peewit, isn't it? Now. (*He imitates a pack of dogs barking. Brings out another bird.*) Nothing like it in England. Sounds like a pack of dogs in full chase.

He does the sound again, intrigued. FitzRoy winces.

Now, where have I put it –

FitzRoy Please! Stop it!

Darwin FitzRoy? Are you unwell.

FitzRoy I am perfectly fit!

Darwin I was so delighted with my discoveries I did not think to ask –

FitzRoy That is not unusual –

Darwin You have been working very hard.

FitzRoy Yes. Mr Geographer, while you were gallivanting about the countryside, I have measured, remeasured, and measured again every inch of this coast. Back and forth, back and forth – there will no error in the charts of these waters.

Darwin Isn't that good?

FitzRoy Good, but not good enough. I have to do it again.

Darwin FitzRoy!

FitzRoy I don't expect you to understand the quest for perfection.

Darwin I am remiss for asking to take an interest in these fossils.

FitzRoy Please to remember I was the first to notice bones embedded in the silt off Punta Alta. Had it not been for me, you wouldn't even know of these animals. (*He puts his hands to his head.*)

Darwin FitzRoy?

FitzRoy Headaches.

Pause.

Darwin I found the country as hospitable as you described it, FitzRoy, but the Spaniards do not have anything like the sophistication of our English landowners. I also felt much disturbed by their policy of killing all the Indians and sending their children into slavery.

FitzRoy I once questioned a landowner on that very subject. He called in twenty of his slaves and asked them what they thought and to a man they said slavery was a good thing.

Darwin What else could they say in front of a man who could put them to death?

FitzRoy Are you questioning my judgement?

Darwin I am surprised you believed them.

FitzRoy But then your grandfather campaigned against slavery, I had forgotten.

Darwin What is wrong with that?

FitzRoy The trouble with meddlers like Wedgwood and other Whigs is that they do not know how other countries work. I do not say we should have slavery in England, but here –

Darwin If something is unjust and inhumane surely it is so everywhere.

FitzRoy It is a subject you do not understand.

Darwin I have travelled and I find slavery abhorrent and degrading.

FitzRoy You seem to take pleasure in contradicting me. (*He holds his head.*)

Darwin FitzRoy, you are not well . . .

FitzRoy It is the headaches that drove my uncle to suicide, he was never mad, whatever they said at your dinner tables – dinner tables . . . yes . . . the dinner we had at the Governor's house. I said everyone was reading Jane Austen. You demurred!

Darwin I only meant there may be some who do not read her.

FitzRoy You contradicted me in public.

Darwin But many Englishmen do not know how to read!

FitzRoy Everyone one knows or cares to know reads Jane Austen, Mr Darwin.

Darwin That is not everyone.

FitzRoy Again! You will drive me mad! I wanted the company of a gentleman. I find I am messing with a man who does not even know how to tidy himself before entering the cabin of his captain.

Darwin I forgot. I am sorry.

FitzRoy From now on, Mr Darwin, I shall have to ask you to mess with the junior officers.

Darwin FitzRoy, you are out of sorts – you –

FitzRoy You will not speak to your captain in this manner! Get out of my cabin and take your disgusting specimens with you. (*He kicks a bone. It disintegrates.*)

SCENE NINE: 'FEAR'

Tom, Ian and Millie.

Millie (*to Tom*) Perfect! How do you do it? I kiss you.

Tom shrugs and takes out a computer game.

(*to Ian*) Yes, but bigger, stronger, more passionate, more desperate, more fearful, more dark.

Tom gets very absorbed in his computer game.

Tom Pchhh –

Millie 'Take your disgusting specimens with you' – symbol of everything he fears.

Ian (*icy*) Are you showing me how to say it?

Millie That bitter reference to Whigs, the Reform Bill giving all these people the vote. Darwin belongs to those upstarts now ruling England.

Ian I know all that.

Millie The Admiralty is angry with FitzRoy for buying a second ship and makes him sell it again, his world is shrinking, he's out of joint so, fear, that terrible icy fear when the climate begins to change, a long winter sets in, I've seen it, at first surprise, then disbelief, then you attack each other because there's not enough food to go around, times of betrayal, despair. And the ice advances towards you.

Ian Could you be specific?

Millie Fear, Ian, it's an English word, no? Contemporary. Daily. Why do you repress that, too?

Tom (*on his computer*) Sitting ducks.

Millie When I saw you for this, I saw that fear. I found out you hadn't worked for a long time.

Ian Through the Bulgarian Secret Police?

Millie Yes, we had to learn in Bulgaria to read a teacher's face to know whether she was teaching us something true or something she'd been told to say, so I can read faces, yes.

Ian The lines are precise, they do not describe a nuclear winter.

Millie But the writer knows social history and the struggle for existence and the world we're in. You're good at something, the climate shrinks your space, you shiver.

Ian Ask the writer to come and tell me on what line he wants me to act the fear of a species facing a cold winter. (*He begins to leave.*)

Millie He's afraid.

Ian leaves.

Tom Zap!

Millie (*to Tom*) Why don't you ever say anything? What do you believe?

Tom Nothing.

Millie In general. God, dialectical materialism, existentialism –

Tom Please, I'm English.

Millie For yourself, even: recognition, money?

Tom I wouldn't be here.

Millie The environment? That's not too mentally taxing.

Tom I like underground car parks. As a child, I loved to stand behind cars and breathe in the fumes, must have been a high.

Millie A psychologist would say you have a vanishing complex, you're afraid to declare you're there. The Alice in Wonderland syndrome. I suppose that's quite English.

Tom I saw the cartoon. I thought Alice was American.

Millie Are you saying you are cynical, selfish, stupid, immoral and want only a good life?

Tom I'm tired of everyone trying to enlist me in their ideas, communism, free marketism, Europe, God, the greatness of science, the purity of art . . . I don't want to be told that this idea is the best idea that ever existed and that I have to fight for it, lose my job for it, even leaflet for it. When I see an idea floating around, about to get stuck on my jacket, I move.

Millie What about culture?

Tom Who?

Millie Here. This. I believe more in this country than you do.

Tom Yeah, that's normal, you're a foreigner. Are you going to stay?

Millie If I can. Stay and be part of it. More British than the British.

Tom You speak so well.

Millie I just get the thoughts wrong. But my accent is good?

Tom Don't lose the passion in your vowels.

Millie They may tell me to go. It depends on this. I have to prove I have something unique to contribute. I'm afraid of the post in the morning, the letter telling me to go home – I have no home.

Tom I'll marry you if you want.

Millie I thought you were –

Tom I am, I can still marry you – if it helps.

Millie What would you –?

Tom Get out of it? I don't believe in profit either.

Millie But why?

Tom There doesn't always have to be a why. When I go out at night, sometimes I take a tube into the centre, sometimes I walk in the woods. I don't know who I'm going to meet. Whether I'll come back alone or with someone, whether it'll be good or not. I could meet the love of my life, or – yeah – maybe death. If I marry you, maybe you'll give me lots of jobs, everybody wants to work with Eastern European directors, maybe they won't next year . . . The offer's open anyway.

Millie kisses Tom gently on the forehead.

Millie You know, in Eastern Europe we are very homophobic.

Tom I've noticed.

Millie I've shown it?

Tom You've shown fear.

Millie A woman's territory is already so insecure.

Tom I love women.

Millie Really?

Tom No, not really. But I do like your vowels.

Millie I can't pass for British unless I get rid of them.

Tom What a sacrifice.

Millie Not for survival.

Tom (*correcting the 'u' of survival*) Survival.

Millie Survival. I still can't believe in generosity without idealism.

Tom That's because you're homophobic. How do you think we survive?

SCENE TEN: 'IDEALISM'

1832. Tierra del Fuego, off the Straits of Magellan.
Rain. Grey. Very cold.
Several boxes are stacked in FitzRoy's cabin, making it even smaller.
FitzRoy and Darwin, cold, having been stuck at sea for a month, drink tea in irritated silence. Every slurp and swallow is self-conscious and intensely heard by the other. Darwin, seasick as usual, swallows frequently, to the annoyance of FitzRoy.
FitzRoy takes ages to put his cup down after a drink, meticulously, silently. Darwin watches, mesmerized, FitzRoy's slightly prissy gestures. Darwin's cup tends to crash a little. FitzRoy winces when that happens as when Darwin clears his throat.
At last tea is over. FitzRoy moves a tray carefully and looks at the skylight.

FitzRoy We have another hour of light.

Darwin looks up, despondent.

Darwin Will the sun never shine?

Darwin takes out some papers and spreads them. FitzRoy moves them slightly back. Darwin doesn't notice and pushes them out again.

FitzRoy In his log book, Captain Stokes described Tierra del Fuego as the dreariest landscape on earth, utterly desolate, where the soul dies – (*Pause.*) He had encountered the sorts of winds we've had, couldn't move for months. Eventually he locked himself in his cabin and shot himself. (*Pause.*) He made rather a mess of it and it took him days to die. When I took over *The Beagle*, the crew kept seeing his ghost, sometimes I think I see his shadow – just there, to your right – (*He stares and moves towards the area indicated, then stops himself.*) But I have a very cheerful task in hand. The good ladies of the Walthamstow missionary society entrusted these boxes to my especial care.

Darwin looks briefly and goes back to his papers.

We'll soon deposit Matthews and the Fuegians – there are some beautiful glaciers in the channel by the way. (*He puts a box on the table, begins to unwrap it.*) I'll make a note of all the items given and the Fuegians will learn to write their own thank-you notes in good time.

Darwin I never thought to see men and women in such an abject state.

FitzRoy They are human beings.

Darwin I feel closer to these beetles.

FitzRoy They will be educated.

Darwin The nakedness, filth, ugliness, shouting, constant begging, (*he imitates*) 'Yamaschooner, yamaschooner –' Is it true that when their women become old, they eat them?

FitzRoy Only in times of famine. I asked Jemmy Button why they didn't eat their dogs instead and he told me it was because the dogs catch otters, but the women can no longer help feed the tribe.

Darwin And you plan to educate them?

FitzRoy Not one of God's creatures is beyond salvation. Try to be a little more charitable, Darwin.

Darwin They repel me.

Darwin goes back to his papers. FitzRoy unwraps some silver-plated cutlery. He counts.

FitzRoy Thirty-six forks, thirty-six spoons, ah, thirty-six fish knives.

Darwin Surely, FitzRoy?

FitzRoy continues doggedly, writing down.

FitzRoy Four serving spoons. (*He unwraps an elegant soup tureen.*) Wedgwood! (*He now unwraps several immaculate, white, embroidered antimacassars.*)

Darwin Antimacassars!

FitzRoy Why not?

Darwin FitzRoy, they've never even seen a blanket –

FitzRoy Why should a Fuegian not sit one day, his hair cut, washed, smoothed with macassar oil, in a huge arm-chair reading a paper? And then his wife shall want anti-macassars. Not immediately perhaps . . . agriculture must be established, basic building skills, weaving – Matthews will hold some of these back, but look how quickly Jemmy Button has learned civilized manners.

Darwin Might he not be happier staying in England? He's such a dandy.

FitzRoy York Minster, the sweet young Fuegia Basket and Jemmy Button will convince these people of the benefits of civilization.

Darwin They will need the oratorical powers of a Marc Anthony.

FitzRoy My greatest ambition is to be remembered as someone who benefited mankind. Is it not yours?

Darwin shrugs.

Lack of ambition is not a fault in a clergyman, Darwin, but you seem harsh towards other human beings. Science may uncover the immutable laws of nature, but man alone has the freedom to change and perfect himself.

Darwin I would not be in Matthews' place for the world.

FitzRoy He trusts in God.

Darwin God help him.

FitzRoy God will. (*He continues to unpack.*) Ten baby bonnets. (*He now begins to unwrap another large object.*) What can this be?

FitzRoy carefully unwraps a large, ornate, Victorian chamber pot. Darwin bursts out laughing.

SCENE ELEVEN: 'IDENTITY'

Tom, Ian, Millie and Lawrence.
Lawrence is black, well dressed in a casual American way. He speaks slowly, in a well-modulated east coast–mid-Atlantic accent.

Lawrence In November 1832, FitzRoy landed his three Fuegians with the missionary Matthews at Ponsonby Sound. Jemmy Button recognized his tribe, but could no longer speak his own language. His mother and his brothers refused to acknowledge him. The sailors erected tents and planted a vegetable garden before leaving. FitzRoy went back ten days later to find the goods stolen, the vegetable garden trampled and Matthews' life threatened. Matthews was re-embarked but Jemmy Button was left to fulfil FitzRoy's vision of a civilized tribe. When FitzRoy returned to Ponsonby Sound a year later, a lone, naked savage with matted hair and painted face emerged from the mist in a dug-out canoe. With difficulty, pain, FitzRoy recognized Jemmy Button. Jemmy, embarrassed by his nakedness, refused to answer FitzRoy's questions until he had been fully clothed. English and good table manners came haltingly back to him over dinner with his beloved captain and he told a sad tale of abject treatment by his tribe and family. And yet he refused to sail with FitzRoy, insisting this was where he belonged. He undressed, lowered himself into his canoe, vanished. He had adopted Englishness with total enthusiasm, but had then readopted the customs of his tribe with equal commitment, thus becoming perhaps one of the first people to suffer the stresses of biculturalism, a condition which was to reach epidemic proportions in the late twentieth century. Jemmy Button's own tribe is now extinct.

Tom Poor Jemmy Button. I love him so.

Lawrence I've always wanted to say something in a real theatre. It's not the same as a lecture hall.

Ian Why don't you? You have a good voice.

Lawrence I wanted to, when I was at college, but I looked around and I thought, no . . . it's too crowded here, so I majored in biology and English instead.

Tom I never imagined you'd be like this – I thought you'd be –

Lawrence (*urbane*) White?

Tom Young – I mean – I've never done a new play before but isn't the writer supposed to wear black leather and get drunk and throw coffee cups around, even if it's a woman, you know –? I don't see you in black leather, Lawrence.

Lawrence Sorry.

Ian Why don't you write yourself a part: Jemmy Button?

Lawrence It's FitzRoy I'm interested in.

Tom FitzRoy!

Lawrence Playwrights are the anatomists of the failed character.

Tom Yeah . . . Right.

Lawrence Not that I presume – this is my first time.

Ian Millie said you were afraid to come . . .

Millie I presumed . . . to guess.

Lawrence I know how prejudiced you are in this country – against Americans. (*to Ian*) I saw you ten years ago. Richard the Second. If someone had told me then – I am a happy man! Sometimes I can't believe this is real.

Tom Yeah . . . I can't take it too seriously myself.

Lawrence It's serious all right, but I'm a teacher as well, a professor, our students have a year abroad – I make sure I'm the tutor as often as possible. Everybody wants to come to England, so I only get here every two or three years. I love it, oh, do I love it here.

Tom Why?

Lawrence Because your pavements burn with history.

Tom They do?

33

Millie Lawrence, do you want to watch some more? I am being very brilliant, I think.

Lawrence A few minutes, then I'm taking my students to the National Portrait Gallery – I teach a course called the Metaphysics of Cultural Genealogy.

SCENE TWELVE: 'CRUELTY'

September 1835. The Galapagos.
Change of light. Heat. Darwin and FitzRoy. Lawrence and Millie, watching.

Darwin Dismal heaps of broken lava . . . hideous lizards with the faces of ancient demons. No wonder sailors couldn't wait to get away.

FitzRoy Los Encantadas, the enchanted isles. The currents are so strong, the islands can vanish overnight and leave you lost in the ocean. I prefer the name Galapagos.

Darwin I see we have six live ones on board.

FitzRoy They'll keep us in meat until Tahiti.

Darwin FitzRoy . . . the governor told me he can recognize which island a tortoise comes from by its markings . . . you know they can't swim . . .

Short pause.

FitzRoy I gather you didn't find much else of interest.

Darwin A few miserable weeds, finches, mocking-birds. Again, quite remarkable differences between them . . . I wonder . . .

FitzRoy, I did something thoroughly foolish: I put all my finches in the same bag.

34

FitzRoy I labelled mine according to each island.

Darwin You are the true naturalist!

FitzRoy I'll give them to you – now you will forgive me – I have some calculations to do – I fell behind – you will forgive me – drudgery calls.

FitzRoy waits for Darwin to go, Darwin ignores him.

Darwin May I show you something?

Darwin takes out some drawings. FitzRoy takes them.

FitzRoy Finches. Quite well drawn. Mine are more precise. (*He hands the drawings back and waits for Darwin to go.*)

Darwin You see how different the beaks are.

FitzRoy Presumably they eat different foods.

Darwin Precisely.

FitzRoy Each one is perfectly adapted to its place in the world, according to the wisdom of God.

Darwin How far are we from the coast of South America?

FitzRoy Five hundred miles. Now, Darwin –

Darwin Don't some of these remind you of birds we saw in South America?

FitzRoy They look like variations, yes.

Darwin Extreme variations.

FitzRoy Perhaps. Darwin, I must ask you –

Darwin Does it not occur to you, FitzRoy, that possibly some of these variations might be so extreme as to constitute – shall we say – a species –?

FitzRoy It is sometimes hard to tell.

Darwin Suppose, only suppose that these volcanic islands emerged from the sea, as Lyell suggests, seeds drifted from South America, clung to the lava providing meagre vegetation – birds followed, settled, dropped more seeds. Suppose that in this strange, this brave new world, isolated from the rest of the continent, the islands, themselves isolated from each other – suppose there began to emerge birds so different from their forebears – look at the beaks, FitzRoy – that they must, in truth, be called a – new – species.

FitzRoy New.

Darwin New . . .

FitzRoy Stop. I see where you are going.

Darwin I do not see myself. Something is at work, but I do not know what.

FitzRoy The devil is at work, here, in this cabin! (*He brushes something away.*) This shadow . . . Darwin, I know the dark night of the soul. Doubt sweeps in like a treacherous wind and puts out God's light. I sat here for days, you heard, with this gun – (*He takes the gun and shows it to Darwin.*) – held to my head – I gave up command of the ship – you weren't here –

Darwin I didn't know. I was very ill. I would have come back.

FitzRoy Wickham saw me through. But sometimes I feel that if I turn my head this way, just a little, then all life will jangle into meaninglessness. Darwin, let me keep you from the vision of a tormented world from which God is absent. I am well now – I have sworn always to keep in sight the divine designer. You too must swear to shut out all the thoughts you have expressed here –

Darwin I don't know what my thoughts are, how can I order them?

36

FitzRoy Let me be their captain, let me steer us both away from madness.

FitzRoy holds out an arm to turn Darwin. Lawrence stops them.

Lawrence Something's missing.

Millie It's fine, Lawrence.

Lawrence How do you excavate the intimate moments of historical characters?

Tom What a fuss over words. What does it matter whether something's a variation or a species?

Lawrence (*picking up and studying the gun*) New. One word. 'New' species.

Millie You can be short, tall, fat, blond or brown, short beaked or long beaked, but if the species were not created but slowly evolved, then nothing is fixed –

Tom So.

Millie You thrive on disorder, Tom, but these two men have been living in a fixed universe. God, man, England, class. If, as Darwin suspects, it is fluid, unplanned, then it is a world without a designer, without God. Lawrence?

Lawrence (*looking at the gun*) Do you think that in a play a gun always has to go off?

Tom I know about evolution, well, sort of, but I pray to God all the time. You know: 'Please God, don't let me catch pneumonia, please make Ian and Lawrence admire me, please make me famous.'

Millie When I was in Sofia I used to go to the Alexander Nevsky cathedral, and in the smokey hues of grey and red I could cry and find hope again, but I had left my rational mind on the steps outside. We read the Bible as metaphor.

Lawrence (*still with the gun*) Some believe access to metaphor is an evolutionary tool to stave off the grief of chaos. We need it more and more.

Tom Yeah. Right. Lawrence, you're a real help.

Ian I don't believe, I never have, but when I am working, like this, I feel what can only be described as a kind of grace.

Millie Yes, yes, it is work! It is work! We will dispel the darkness: we will work! Ian, I begin to love you!

Ian (*to Lawrence*) Is it FitzRoy's hereditary madness that's coming over me?

Lawrence There's a genetic predisposition from the family, a cultural one from Captain Stokes, and the environment is right. If you go for only one of those options you'll destroy the mystery of being human.

Millie To suggest the words of the Bible are not literally true and no longer hold the world safe, there is the wreckage – the madness. FitzRoy sees that all sense could crumble in his mind, have you never felt that? You look outside, it's all a jumble and you hear, too – a jumble, words that belong to no language at all – FitzRoy sees – he hears – Darwin as Lucifer, defying God, jumbling the creation. And he puts out his hand to hold Darwin back, keep him fixed. Tom, you turn away, stand there, enchanted by these islands, their possibilities – this new world that came into being so gradually, so accidentally and also – you see this already – so cruelly.

Tom I love the cruelty. Very now. Yes. Let's have more cruelty.

> *They stay in position. Millie watches. Lawrence toys with the gun, then hands it to Ian.*

Act Two

SCENE ONE: 'JEALOUSY'

Darwin's study. Not dissimilar to FitzRoy's cabin in feel, but much messier: a desk crammed with papers. A very comfortable rolling leather chair, books and books. Jars, skeletons.

Millie is still setting some bits up. Ian and Tom say lines quite fast to each other. Millie occasionally listens but keeps changing things on the desk, coming in and out. Ian is intense, Tom quite distracted. Lawrence comes in with a jar of barnacles.

FitzRoy 'Mr Darwin's journal is still detained, to the great regret of the scientific world, because it is to form part of a longer work including an account of the Surveys of Captains King and FitzRoy in South America . . .' And I had been led to believe that the scientific world was waiting for an account by *The Beagle*'s captain. I sent Mr Lyell my chapter on the Deluge for his comments, I am still waiting. Presumably he cannot answer. Have you read it?

Darwin I found the arguments difficult.

FitzRoy I put them succinctly.

Darwin I am a naturalist, not a theologian.

FitzRoy Your own mentor Sedgwick has repeatedly said that scientific truths are there to reveal God's intentions. I *prove* the truth of revelation. I even use some of your finds. Indeed, Darwin, I mention you often.

Darwin I am flattered.

FitzRoy You seem to have forgotten it was by my invitation you joined *The Beagle*.

Darwin I cannot imagine my life without those five years!

FitzRoy My officers were kind to you. They could have been handsomely rewarded if they had collected their own specimens. They made room for you instead.

Darwin The specimens are even more interesting than I knew, FitzRoy!

FitzRoy Please give me their names.

Millie Please *to* give me their names. It's an interesting English construction.

FitzRoy Please to give me their names.

Darwin Many don't have names yet.

FitzRoy The names of my officers!

Darwin FitzRoy!

FitzRoy The names!

Darwin Sulivan, Usborne.

Tom What are their names?

Ian Wickham . . .! Come on, Tom.

Darwin Wickham, Stewart, need I go on?

FitzRoy You talk of sunsets, plants, generals, but never a mention of these superb officers – even I, your captain, hardly feature at all.

Darwin I shall endeavour to repair the omission.

FitzRoy nods. Pause.

FitzRoy You are getting married?

Millie I had almost forgotten! (*She goes out.*)

Darwin To my cousin Emma Wedgwood.

FitzRoy You must be patient. It takes at least six months to find happiness in marriage. Perhaps she will bring you back on to the path from which you have strayed.

Darwin No doubt she will try.

FitzRoy I am concerned by a line in your account, which you will notice I have read with great care. You propose the Galapagos Islands were originally under water, that is consistent with my chapter on the Deluge, but you then go on to say, and you will forgive me if I have not memorized it correctly: 'Hence, both in space and time, we seem to be brought a little nearer to that great fact – the mystery of mysteries – the first appearance of new beings on Earth.'

Darwin You are word perfect, FitzRoy. Should it be 'a little nearer'?

Ian I've just said 'a little nearer'.

Tom Is it important?

Ian You say, 'should it be somewhat nearer.' You've got to get this right!

Tom 'Should it be somewhat nearer.' Is this really important?

Millie comes in with a portrait.

Millie Your wife. Very pretty in a dull sort of English way. Do you like her? I am so excited, you are two such wonderful men. I love you. I envy you.

Lawrence comes in with large jars.

And Lawrence has brought some more barnacles.

Lawrence I'll teach you to dissect them.

Millie Tom, you have terrible stomach problems. And the age, yes? And Ian, for you, it's what's called being ill at ease in your skin, it's too tight maybe – or askew . . . (*She demonstrates on Ian's arm, stares at him for a moment. She goes out.*)

FitzRoy It does not matter whether it is a little nearer or somewhat nearer. You agreed on the ship to abandon such thoughts.

Darwin I can think what I want on dry land. (*to Lawrence*) I don't remember Darwin agreeing to anything.

FitzRoy Not if you are a gentleman.

Lawrence Something happened between them in the Galapagos, but I haven't discovered it yet.

FitzRoy You are beginning to make a reputation for yourself, Darwin, but if you make public the thoughts you confessed to me, you will be ostracized. And I shall feel responsible for the misery you bring to yourself. I was your captain, Darwin.

Darwin That was five years ago.

FitzRoy Three. I hope I may consider myself your friend.

Lawrence I've got to go and do some more work. It's important.

Tom Is it?

Lawrence leaves.

FitzRoy I want to protect you.

A bleep goes off. Ian looks for something.

Darwin Captain FitzRoy, you will have to allow me to look after myself.

FitzRoy Can you?

Darwin Very well.

Another beep goes off. Ian takes out a Tamagotchi and presses a few buttons.

Ian My daughter's Tamagotchi. She comes every other weekend and I look after it the rest of the time. If something happens, she'll never trust me again.

Tom and Ian both look.

I think it wants to be fed. (*He gently hands the Tamagotchi to Tom.*) A virtual baby. You get very attached.

Tom quickly hands it back.

Tom So: is it important?

The Tamagotchi bleeps again. Ian looks at it.

Ian What?

Tom This . . . Darwin . . . evolution.

Ian That is rather important.

Tom They talk, that's all they do, talk. Even the government is saying we don't need this any more. If they had a shoot-out now – pcchhhh.

Tom imitates a gun fight. The Tamagotchi goes off again.

Ian What do you want now? They're easily bored.

Tom Admit it, you'd love to make a film.

Ian If it was good, maybe.

Tom Even if it was bad, come on.

Ian Fifteen years ago, I was doing a good line of parts and the theatre seemed a noble, solid, even impregnable environment. This young, hot American director came to

England and suddenly decided he wanted me in his film. He took me out to breakfast and laid before me the promise of stardom, wealth, power – I was dazed. As an afterthought, he gave me the script. It was about a serial murderer.

Tom Pchhh. Pchhh.

Ian His increasing skill at not getting caught. The path of such a character in Shakespeare or Ibsen would reaffirm a moral environment –

The Tamagotchi goes off.

(*to the Tamagotchi*) Wait. I'm talking. Not here. Nothing. I turned it down. I was sure the film wouldn't have an audience. When it came out, it was a huge success and for the first time I felt the icy trickle of fear – as if the ornate skills I was developing would soon be redundant, like the ten-foot antlers of the Irish elk which killed him when he kept getting stuck in the trees.

Tom Absolutely. No antlers for me. You can do both.

Ian You have to be very lucky or very stupid to survive in two environments at once.

Tom So my stupidity could be – what's the word – a modern adaptation.

Ian Too many film stars give bad performances. It's not that they've lost their talent, but their sense of self.

Tom Yeah, but they're eating lots of food in the meantime.

Ian I tell myself nobody knows ahead of time which species will survive. Those first little mammals looked unpromising.

Tom You don't sound convinced. Look how pinched you are – like FitzRoy.

The Tamagotchi goes off.

Ian Drink? Sleep?

Tom You see, I've been checked again.

Ian Nappy? What?

Tom For that film. Pchhh. Pchhh. It's not a German accent, it's euh – Balkan – that's Millie's patch, isn't it?

Ian Is that better?

Tom It's between me and this other guy. It would start in a week's time, so I'd have to leave this.

Ian Well, you can't

Tom Actually, I can.

The Tamagotchi goes off. Ian shakes it.

Ian (*to the Tamagotchi*) Let me talk to Tom! It's jealous. You're not serious.

Tom I'm hungry, Ian, I want to go where there's lots of food.

Ian You have a contract.

Tom Paper. Millie can't take me to court.

Ian One doesn't do that.

Tom You don't. I do.

Ian Tom, you cannot do this – morally.

Tom I don't understand that word, Ian.

Ian makes to seize Tom, violently.

Tom Pchhh. Pchhh. Use words, Ian, go ahead. Convince me.

Ian You're not some animal foraging for food.

Tom That's what Darwin's saying here, isn't it?

Ian You're part of a culture that nurtured you, that gives you your identity and protects you from despair. You're playing a man of extreme decency and you're taking the most superficial reading of his own words to excuse your disgusting, criminal, your tawdry –

Tom Come on, come on.

Ian You've formed relationships here, to Millie, to me, to Lawrence – how many black writers do you know? He's American, OK, but he can spawn cultural descendants here. You have an obligation and you do know what that word means because under that camouflage of idiocy is a man of talent who somewhere, however dimly, believes, believes, yes – oh my God, I don't know what to say – Give me time. Please.

The Tamagotchi goes off. Ian ignores it.

Tom Sure. If you promise not to say anything to Millie, just in case it doesn't work out.

Ian Millie might just be able to find someone else – no, it wouldn't be any good. Damn you!

Tom Promise.

Ian You won't agree to anything without asking me?

Tom It's a deal.

The Tamagotchi bleeps insistently.

Ian It's got a fever. They can die, you know.

SCENE TWO: 'TRUTH'

1843. Down house, Kent.
Darwin's study. Papers, books, jars. Children's toys.
FitzRoy, seemingly aged, and Darwin.

FitzRoy You did not answer my last letter, but I have come down to Kent nonetheless. I've come to say goodbye. I am being made governor of New Zealand.

Darwin I must congratulate you.

FitzRoy There has been trouble between the settlers and the Maoris and they want someone to calm the situation.

Darwin looks dubiously at FitzRoy, then distracts himself with one of his jars. FitzRoy looks around.

You seem comfortable here. Your study reminds me a little of my cabin.

Darwin is increasingly absorbed by his jar. FitzRoy eventually picks one up as well.

Barnacles. I'm pleased to see you are homesick for *The Beagle*.

Darwin Do you remember the new *Balanus arthrobalanus* I found in Chile? I've decided to take on the whole genus. Let me show you something. (*He takes out a barnacle and dissects quickly and expertly.*) Here is a female and what's this on her?

FitzRoy looks.

Twelve males. They have no mouth, no stomach, no thorax, no limbs, no abdomen. They consist wholly of reproductive organs in an envelope.

FitzRoy Fascinating.

Darwin My children find it very funny.

FitzRoy You show this to your children!

Darwin They run in and out all the time. Annie already helps me catalogue.

47

FitzRoy May I assume you are leaving those – other thoughts behind you.

Darwin These barnacles will take me years.

Brief pause.

FitzRoy I only ever wanted good to come to the world.

Darwin says nothing.

I am haunted by the sight of Jemmy Button. Did I fail him? I am a man of honour and integrity. How can the values I uphold have become untrue? I wanted the world to savour God through your findings. The truth cannot be as cruel as you suggested. We could not live with that truth. I failed Jemmy's tribe, don't let me fail the world, Darwin.

Darwin My little barnacles won't do much one way or the other.

FitzRoy They can show order and the beauty of the creation. (*He grabs hold of Darwin in an uncharacteristic gesture.*) Because it's there, Darwin, isn't it? It's there. (*He keeps shaking Darwin.*) It's there. It's there. It's there.

Millie comes on and gently disengages Ian.

Millie Ian . . .

Ian It's there, isn't it. Isn't it. Isn't it.

Millie (*quickly*) In the next scene, Darwin has written the most important book of the modern world. (*to Tom*) You have read it.

Tom shakes his head.

I ordered you to read it!

Tom I got put off by the pigeons. My idea of Hell is walking through the pigeons of Trafalgar Square.

Millie Go to the next chapter.

Tom I'll lose the plot. A friend is bringing me the video.

Millie Of what?

Tom Of the Origin of Species. It's only an hour. And it has close-ups of important words, you know, like selection, and some nice animals. I can fast-forward the pigeons.

Millie When I interviewed you you said you were interested in evolution.

Tom I wanted the job.

Millie How dare you lie to me! And tell me only now when it is too late to get rid of you!

Tom I don't have to be Darwin to act Darwin.

Millie You have to understand every word he says.

Tom Do you?

Millie Of course, I've read all of Darwin.

Ian All of Darwin?

Millie Tom, I will sit with you every evening and read to you, you will like it.

Tom That's my body time . . .

Ian (*over*) When did you read all of Darwin? There's yards of him.

Millie It is sexy.

Ian Where?

Millie I am talking to Tom about evolution!

Ian We're both interested in your evolution. Aren't we Tom?

Millie I do not have time to tell you. (*to Tom*) Now I will have to teach you evolution. I will start with plants. Ian, you may go.

Ian I want to learn.

Millie It's not important for you.

Ian Where did you learn about Darwin?

Millie In the Bulgarian theatre. We are very intelligent.

Ian They teach evolution in drama school?

Millie Yes.

Tom Wow.

Millie Why not? The esssence of drama is conflict, no? Struggle: evolution.

Ian And it's taught to opera singers as well, ballet dancers . . . makes them leap higher?

Millie All right. I learned about Darwin in High School. Now Tom –

Ian Clearly you were a brilliant pupil . . .

Millie I wanted to come to England and study science.

Tom Wow.

Ian Wouldn't that have been better?

Tom A lot of intelligent people go into the theatre, there's nothing wrong with that.

Ian It can be the wrong choice.

Millie Evolution does not explain the suicidal gesture.

Ian That's a good definition of going into the theatre. It still doesn't explain you.

Tom You've been lying to us . . . about Moscow . . .

Millie In the 1960s Zhivkov decreed that members of the Communist Party must be pure Bulgarians. So my family, which had had a Turkish name since the middle ages, changed it to a Bulgarian one. They also found a monk in Rila monastery who was willing, for a fee, to become a close cousin – so I was born into a respected medical family of pure and ancient Bulgarian origin. In my last year of high school, I stumbled on the truth, and I don't know why, I really don't know why, I decided to proclaim my Turkish identity. It was just when they were confiscating the property of anyone with a Turkish name, so I was immediately expelled – my parents went into hiding. I had never been political, I did not have the dissident's art of survival. I drifted to the capital, I found a job at the theatre.

Ian As a director?

Millie As a cleaner. When the communists fell, I took back my Bulgarian name, but it was too late to go to university. I came here and implied I was a director who had worked as a cleaner. You were so romantic about us, no one asked questions. And also I had fallen in love – with this – maybe because – maybe it could explain my suicidal gesture. I took an English name.

Ian Millie.

Millie Amelia.

Ian Why didn't you tell us before?

Millie The truth is not a good survival tool. It makes you vulnerable . . .

Ian And so attractive . . .

Ian and Millie stare at each other for a moment.

Millie I can become good at this, I know I can become good at this, I will work and work and become good at this – and then at last I will be safe.

SCENE THREE: 'THE ORIGIN OF SPECIES'

1857. Darwin's study.
   More things: nests, lots of books, portraits of several children.
   The men have aged.

Darwin I am not certain: Natural Selection . . . The Struggle for Existence . . . The Origin of Species.

FitzRoy And you will say that God did not create permanent species.

Darwin I say every species multiplies at an unsustainable rate. There is not enough food, hence competition, any individual who has an advantage over another –

FitzRoy Advantage given to it by God.

Darwin More like accident. The advantage is not immediately evident, but it gives the individual a better chance of finding food, a stronger beak will crack harder berries, let us say – and the advantageous trait is inherited by the offspring and this leads gradually to the formation of a new species, especially in isolated geographical areas like the Galapagos – if you remember –

FitzRoy I remember that time better than you!

Darwin The changes take place over millions of years, like the formation of our Earth.

FitzRoy And man?

Darwin That will be another book.

FitzRoy That is what everyone will want to know.

Darwin He too evolved.

FitzRoy That is not possible.

Darwin I believe it is the truth.

FitzRoy You do not have to publish your misguided beliefs.

Darwin I was sent a paper by a young man called Alfred Russel Wallace: all my ideas are there, FitzRoy.

FitzRoy Never heard of him. No one will listen to what he says, but you are respected in the best circles – let this Wallace publish.

Darwin It came to him in a three-day fever –

FitzRoy Quite –

Darwin I have spent twenty years working it out. I would have to let another man . . . another man . . .

FitzRoy Are you saying you are publishing out of the vilest personal ambition?

  Millie comes on.

Millie I do not believe you are desperate enough to publish this book!

Tom I understand exactly how he feels. It would be like letting someone else have a film part, even if it's going to hurt people. Even nice Mr Darwin wants fame. It's natural. So I was right to do it.

Ian You've accepted? You promised!

Tom I was afraid you'd convince me, so I acted first.

Millie (*over them*) Tom, you must read *The Origin*, or the audience will know you are stupid.

Tom I can't do anything about my genes!

Ian He's not stupid, just duplicitous.

Tom Yeah, my dad was like that.

Millie Here's Lawrence, maybe he can convince you.

Tom Lawrence, oh God.

Lawrence comes on with pages.

Ian (*to Tom*) You mean, 'Oh genes.'

Lawrence You know that gun?

Ian Tom has something to say. Find the words, Tom.

Tom Easy: I've accepted a film part, I start next week.

Millie That's when we start. (*Pause.*) You cannot do it. That would be immoral.

Tom Yeah, I know, but I have.

Ian In contemporary Britain, Millie, the moral dilemma is an overspecialized refinement that leads rapidly to extinction.

Tom (*to Lawrence*) I like Darwin, I'm sorry.

Lawrence Does that mean I can make you change your mind?

Tom No, it means, well, it doesn't mean anything, it's what you say when you feel bad; I'm used to feeling bad.

Millie It is the end of everything. All this: wreckage, ashes, nothingness.

Tom You can start again.

Millie You stupid boy, who will give me the chance? I begged, I cajoled for this, now, you know, no violence, not much sex, history, ideas, no one's going to photograph Lawrence naked to the waist, but we found a small and secure space – and I am so very tired and it is such a struggle –

Lawrence Millie, take it easy . . .

Millie Easy? What do you know, you American, you have oil in your country, you grow wheat. I thought to myself I could thrive in the West because I have something you do not have – intellectual energy and passion, too – but now I see it is a disadvantage and I will go home and if I die of hunger at least I will know why. But I cannot understand you, Tom. I come from a culture where many of us had to do terrible things, but you do not have to do this.

Lawrence I think I understand him. If you are in a threatened environment, you have to be prepared to jump.

Millie I do not understand you either, why don't you beat him up or something male or something? I am an intelligent being, I do not want to go extinct, but I do. I am going to sleep, right now.

Ian Millie, we can start again.

Millie The letter came yesterday. I am an economic migrant. I have lived in the spare rooms of those who found eastern Europe exotic, but we are becoming less fashionable and the rooms have got smaller and the effort – even to dress well – and the round at the pub which means no lunch, no supper –

Ian Why didn't you say?

Millie I will not have you feel sorry for me. Never! I am a Bulgarian! I only say this because I am going tomorrow. Today. Now. I need a phone. Why doesn't anybody have a mobile phone. What kind of actors are you!

Tom I could still marry you, we could even have children.

I've absorbed enough about this to want to profligate –
promulgate my genes – yours must be great, I mean, all
that Darwin.

*Ian moves quickly to Tom as if to hit him. Lawrence
stops him.*

Lawrence Hey, man . . .

Ian storms out. Millie lies down and curls up.

Lawrence (*to Tom, gently*) It is quite possible –

Millie Quiet please, I am going extinct.

Lawrence – that human beings have come to the end of
their evolution – some say we are even coming to the end
of our knowledge, who knows, but, Tom, we will never
come to the end of our imagination. When I see a character on stage, I think, ah, where is he going, he's emerged
from the tragic, is he a hybrid, a completely new form?
And I never stop being excited by the human possibilities
– that struggle for existence on this small space – (*Pause.*)
I like film too. Is it a good part?

Tom Yeah, I think so.

Lawrence What do you say, let me hear.

Tom (*with accent*) Line up. Move. Keep moving.

Pause.

Lawrence That's it?

Tom No, I'm in a lot of scenes and there's a close-up of
my face and I go from frightened to excited to completely
blank. My face on the whole screen. I'm interested in
doing blank. You know: nothing. Like: beyond anger.

Lawrence I understand. Tom, I wasn't born into the black
American middle class. It's been a long road.

Tom Lawrence –

Lawrence It's my mother who did it. She worked in one
of these windowless offices in Washington for forty years.
She took me out of school when I was eight – I was beginning to go wild, beyond anger as you say – and she locked
me up with books, everything she could get her hands on.
Here, she said to me, here's your friends, Shakespeare,
Milton, *Moby Dick*, that's the only gang you're ever going
to hang out with. She put in extra hours to hire tutors.
No black writers. No writing on slavery. When I told her
about Caliban she tore out *The Tempest* from my collected Shakespeare. I wouldn't do it to my children, but it
worked, I guess.

Tom Lawrence, I don't do guilt.

Lawrence She's coming over in a couple of days. With
two of her friends from the choir, they've managed to get
the Church to raise the fares.

Tom I'm sorry.

Lawrence She's seventy years old, she's never been to
England. So what I'm saying is, could you keep going
until the end of the week, and I could at least bring her
and her friends?

*Millie curls up tighter. Lawrence takes out money and a
piece of paper.*

And she wants Millie to buy three hats – three English
hats. For the occasion. She says she wants the best. And
one for you. Will five hundred dollars be enough? I've got
the head measurements here.

SCENE FOUR: 'SEXUAL SELECTION'

Ian and Millie.

Ian Tell me about your life in Bulgaria.

Millie We were doing very well for a while. We had expanded to the gates of Constantinople and were ruled with humanity and order by a man called Samuel. One day, an invading army filed into a narrow defile called Cimbalongus. Samuel was taken by surprise and escaped but fifteen thousand of his men were taken prisoner. All of them were blinded except for one man in a hundred who was left with one eye to lead the defeated army back to Samuel. When he saw this, Samuel died of grief and Bulgaria cracked.

Ian Was your family in that army?

Millie Perhaps. It happened in the year one thousand and fourteen. Like most Bulgarians, I feel in my blood the ardent desire for conquest combined with a terrible fear of being blinded. Tell me about being English.

Ian We think of ourselves as restrained and well behaved, and then, suddenly, our natural desires and passions break through and we act on impulse. (*He impulsively moves to Millie and kisses her.*) And then we are surprised and shocked by our actions.

Millie I do not allow this.

Ian Of course . . . and there is someone else . . .

Millie No, but I am your director. I will accept an apology and then I will buy the hats and then we will work.

Ian On what?

Millie Byzantium fell. Bulgaria is still around. We will rehearse and rehearse until Tom leaves us.

Ian Yes.

A pause between them.

Millie I will wait.

Ian For an apology . . .

Millie For the next scene.

SCENE FIVE: 'THE STRUGGLE FOR EXISTENCE'

Down House. Same as previous scene. Darwin and FitzRoy.

Darwin My book is carefully argued. Look at my notes, here – Even so, Wallace and I will give a joint paper and then I will publish. The idea is out, you cannot stop it.

FitzRoy We strive for the good because of our faith. Destroy that and we lose our moral sense and are no better than animals.

Darwin We are no different from animals.

FitzRoy All of my life I have followed moral precepts. It does not bring me advantage, on the contrary. I would have been better liked in New Zealand if I had not wanted the good. You heard.

Darwin I understand there is a book. I have not read it.

FitzRoy Vilifying me for wanting to protect the Maoris. The settlers there are like you, Darwin, they believe only in grabbing more land for themselves because they are stronger. I tried to stop it. They burned my effigy.

Darwin I am sorry.

FitzRoy The noble man does not struggle for advantage. Let us remain noble.

Darwin But the truth.

FitzRoy The common man will misuse the truth, your ideas will be an excuse for every excess.

Darwin I wanted to give up twenty years ago when I first saw – the idea would not let go.

FitzRoy I only ask you not to publish.

Darwin Copernicus and Galileo did not destroy God. Indeed, the notion of God seems to recover quite easily from us men of science.

FitzRoy It does not matter whether the Earth revolves around the Sun or the Sun around the Earth, there is still order and harmony. This is struggle, disorder, despair, horror, chaos. (*He takes out a small Bible from his pocket.*) This is beauty and security. I would have thought that the death of your dear daughter would have brought back your faith.

Darwin (*very dark*) Quite the opposite!

FitzRoy And you want to drag us all into Hell. (*Pause.*) I know what it looks like. Don't think I do not understand your theory. Even see how it could – but I will not allow it to exist. (*He takes out a pistol.*)

Darwin FitzRoy, we have been here before.

FitzRoy I will do it this time.

Darwin The book is already with the publishers.

    Millie and Lawrence come on.

Millie We have to go back to the Galapagos.

Ian Not the Galapagos!

Lawrence Those pages I gave you. I've discovered what happened.

Tom How about FitzRoy is really gay and declares his love for Darwin.

Millie Yes, but it would be repressed. (*to Ian*) You see how I adapt? Now to the Galapagos.

Tom I feel seasick, can't we just go on –

Millie No. Take off your ages, the bitterness and fatigue of life, go back to the light and heat, to FitzRoy's cabin, to the Galapagos –

Tom Millie –

Millie Silence! Be grateful for the chance –

   The Tamagotchi goes off.

I said silence! Give it to me, I'll keep it quiet.

Ian You know about them?

Millie I have one. I do a time share.

SCENE SIX: 'NATURAL SELECTION'

Darwin and FitzRoy. Light.
   Same positions as at end of Act One.
   Lawrence and Millie watch.

Darwin Dismal heaps of broken lava . . . hideous lizards with the faces of ancient demons.

FitzRoy Los Encantadas. I prefer the name Galapagos.

Darwin FitzRoy . . . the governor told me he can recognize which island a tortoise comes from by its markings . . . you know they can't swim . . .

FitzRoy I gather you didn't find much else of interest.

Darwin A few miserable weeds, finches, mockingbirds. Again, quite remarkable differences between them . . . I wonder . . . FitzRoy, may I show you something?

Darwin takes out some drawings. FitzRoy takes them.

FitzRoy Finches. Quite well drawn. Mine are more precise.

Darwin Don't some of these remind you of birds we saw in South America?

FitzRoy They look like variations, yes.

Darwin Extreme variations.

FitzRoy Perhaps. Darwin, I must ask you –

Darwin FitzRoy: suppose, only suppose that these volcanic islands emerged from the sea, as Lyell suggests, seeds drifted from South America, clung to the lava – birds followed, dropped more seeds. Suppose that in this strange, this brave new world, isolated from the rest of the continent, the islands, themselves isolated from each other – suppose there began to emerge birds so different from their forebears – look at the beaks, FitzRoy – that they must, in truth, be called a – new – species.

FitzRoy New.

Darwin New . . .

FitzRoy Stop. I see where you are going.

Darwin I do not see myself. Something is at work, but I do not know what.

FitzRoy The devil is at work, here, in this cabin!

Darwin See the face of nature so bright with gladness, FitzRoy, but we do not see – we forget – that the birds which are singing around us live on insects or seeds and are thus destroying life – and we forget how these birds, or their nestlings or their eggs, are constantly eaten by beasts of prey – it is a cruel world, beak against beak – food is scarce, the one with a tiny advantage – strength maybe or a better disguise, that one will survive – the misfit must perish –

FitzRoy Swear to me you will abandon all such thoughts.

Darwin What if the truth is here?

FitzRoy takes the gun from the table.

FitzRoy I know the dark night of the soul, Darwin. I turned this on myself in my mind's darkness –

Darwin FitzRoy, it would explain all the animals which have disappeared, all those bones I found. The struggle is fierce –

FitzRoy turns the gun on Darwin.

FitzRoy You are the darkness.

Darwin Don't be foolish, FitzRoy, I am only thinking.

FitzRoy Now you will swear to stop.

Darwin Ideas multiply in my mind, they have me in their grip, they eat my rest –

FitzRoy clicks the gun.

FitzRoy Darwin, I will do it.

Darwin sees FitzRoy is serious and goes still.

Darwin FitzRoy, you have not been well.

FitzRoy I felt the brush of the devil. It was you. (*He aims carefully.*)

Darwin You cannot shoot an unarmed man. It is – dishonourable.

63

FitzRoy Men sacrifice their lives – I can damn my soul to save humanity. Swear.

Darwin FitzRoy!

FitzRoy Swear!

Darwin I cannot swear.

FitzRoy Swear.

Darwin I cannot.

FitzRoy On your honour, on the Bible and before God. You will go down on your knees, Darwin, and you will swear never again to think the thoughts you have expressed here. If you cannot, I, who stand here to represent God as the captain of this ship, I will have to kill you.

Darwin hesitates. The gun is aimed. Darwin goes down on his knees.

Darwin I swear.

Pause. Lawrence comes on with Millie.

Lawrence It is a modern play, the gun does not have to go off.

Ian FitzRoy breaks his code by threatening an unarmed man. Darwin is a Victorian gentleman, he swears on the Bible, later he loses his favourite daughter . . . it's grim.

Tom I had to, the idea is like a South American virus, it takes over, digs its claws, multiplies, feeds. It does anything to survive. Yeah. Great. Can we do it my way now? Could you be in love with me?

FitzRoy/Ian You will thank me one day . . . (*He comes close to Darwin and takes him into a very tender embrace.*) I have wanted your good, I have loved you and admired you. Will you forgive me?

Tom I like that.

Ian I meant it. I am asking your forgiveness.

Millie We are coming to FitzRoy's suicide which is seen as an act of madness.

Lawrence In Japanese literature it would be an heroic act because the hero is always on the losing side.

Ian Don't say that or Millie will ask us to do it kabuki style. If I could have this gun rather than a razor it would more tragic.

Lawrence You cannot be tragic after Darwin.

Ian FitzRoy has disappeared from history because he is on the side of the losers, but I see him as a good man who gets it wrong, that is tragic –

Lawrence A new species of modern sadness, perhaps . . .

Tom Yeah, because I'm the hero, I get it right and my idea survives, great. Pchhh. I'm sorry, I'm not doing this for much longer.

Ian You are.

Tom Yeah, for the Baptist Church Choir coming from America.

Lawrence Catholic.

Tom Right – and then L.A.!

Ian (*over all this*) Just a chance, I thought – so I broke my code, like FitzRoy . . . I walked around the streets, there are so many business centres, computers, the internet, e-mail, the rapid breeding of communication.

Millie Ian . . .

Ian So I went into a computer shop –

65

Millie This is not interesting right now.

Ian (*over*) I found Tom's film company on the internet and I e-mailed it. I said I was Tom's lover, that I was HIV positive and that I believed Tom was, too.

Tom But that's a lie.

Ian Even when I was married I told the truth, and yet – it was so easy. Words . . . I elaborated on how you'd recently been unwell . . .

Pause.

Tom You've just ruined my film career.

Ian (*imitating Tom*) Pchhh. I saw a great actor when I was a child. When I met him years later I went over to him and kissed him. You're my father, I said to him, you put me into this world. I never kissed my real father. I want spiritual sons. I'll do what I have to get them. I don't want another two years without work. I want to survive, I want Millie to survive, I want this to survive.

Tom You've destroyed my life!

Millie It's only a delay, Tom, and maybe someone will see you here –

Tom Not with that e-mail. That's it. I don't exist. No one will risk the insurance.

Ian All you have to do is send the results of a recent test.

Tom I've never had a test.

Ian I would have thought –

Tom What would you have thought, Ian? I don't want to know. It's bad enough every time I get the flu, people ring you up, you know, they wait, they don't quite ask –

Lawrence Aren't you putting others at risk?

Tom The only person who's ever at risk is myself, Lawrence.

Ian Oh, my God.

Tom My father died of a heart attack when he was forty, I had a lover who died of AIDS, my best friend was murdered. I'm a modern boy, death lurks there behind the trees, I'm used to that, the only question is what it's going to look like. (*He starts to cry.*)

Millie But the film . . . you might have ended up on the cutting-room floor.

Tom My life's there anyway, in his terms, Darwin's, I would have left my face behind.

Millie Only great films survive, Tom.

Tom You get the video, somebody, some time, would switch me on, even if only to say, he's good looking, where is he now?

Pause.

Ian Where's the gene for shame, Lawrence?

Lawrence In the soul, Ian.

Ian (*to Tom*) I so hated what you did.

Tom Maybe you should learn some humanity.

Ian bows his head.

Millie If people's attention wasn't such a shrinking space we wouldn't be at each other's throat, but it gets smaller and more barren and so we fight. Let's go on.

Lawrence No.

Millie We have to go on.

Lawrence I cannot accept Ian's gesture.

Millie Ian's not asking for your admiration.

Lawrence I mean that I have to refuse. I was brought up a Catholic.

Millie You didn't do anything.

Lawrence I would be colluding.

Millie Well, go to confession and get God to forgive you!

Lawrence He's not so powerful any more – I have to live with my conscience.

Millie The theatre isn't a church, Lawrence, it's a body politic. Look. (*She takes out a well-thumbed book from her bag.*) Machiavelli. I read it every night before I go to sleep.

Tom I love his lyrics, I didn't know he wrote a book.

Lawrence I had a student in a creative writing class once, one of these arrogant, very rich, east-coast kids. First day, he said to me, teach me to write like Kafka. I don't get angry very much, but I did then. Find the man's moral calibre, I said, assume it, and then come back to me. He wasn't stupid, he dropped out of the course. I am responsible for my own integrity.

Millie What about your mother? Isn't she here?

Lawrence If there's one thing a black American woman from Washington D.C. knows, it's the difference between right and wrong.

Millie Tom has nothing else now. He has to do it.

Lawrence I wouldn't allow him to after what Ian's done –

Tom Hey, Lawrence . . . It's my decision.

Lawrence You have to stand up for your principles.

Tom Yeah, but I don't know what they are.

Lawrence I know mine and it's no.

Millie Your principles are going to do nothing but harm.

Lawrence I would not be a happy man.

Millie Your happiness is of no interest to any of us, Lawrence. You're a writer, you should be miserable.

Lawrence I thought you were such nice people, so serious, in this wonderful country of yours. I'm confused now – you don't seem to understand – I'd feel my work was contaminated –

Millie It's not yours any more, it's ours, Ian's, mine. You can go away.

Lawrence I don't think so.

Tom I don't understand you, Lawrence, the person I felt most bothered about when I accepted the film was you – I thought you'd be desperate, beat me up even.

Lawrence Do you have any idea how often a man like me has to resist that impulse? (*Pause.*) This isn't my first disappointment. I'll recover.

Millie And what about us?

Lawrence Find yourselves a light comedy.

Millie Lawrence, I think I am going to have to eliminate you.

Lawrence Don't talk crazy.

Millie I am going crazy, I am about to go completely crazy, and now I am going to start screaming.

Lawrence (*to Ian*) I admired you so much.

Ian What happened to your love for the failed character?

Lawrence I like them kept between the covers of books.

Tom Hey, I'm the victim here. I've lost my future in Hollywood. (*Pause.*) Maybe it's shock, but I don't seem to care. Maybe I don't care about anything. It's your Darwin, Lawrence, he's scrambled my brain. He's turned Ian into moral pus. I've been feeling this virus gripping me. No, not *that* virus, this one. You see, maybe I want to do this, or rather, maybe it wants to use me to do itself. And then even you couldn't say no, Lawrence. I need a walk.

Millie One, two, three, four . . .

Lawrence I'll come with you.

Millie begins to scream.
  Tom and Lawrence go off. Millie stops screaming immediately. Silence. Ian still has his head in his hands, eyes closed. Millie moves very close to him.

Ian Viking, North Utsire, South Utsire, Forties. Did you know FitzRoy originated the shipping forecast?

Millie nods her head.

He was reviled at the time for believing the weather could be predicted. Now we have weather channels. Cromerty, Forth, Tyne, Dogger. They'll come back, won't they? They'll have to.

Millie shrugs.

That's all he has left, but it's not bad is it? And then he looks fine. Fisher, German Bight, Humber, Thames, Dover. Wight. I play the one who gets it wrong. Means well. Does ill. Always. Tragic.

Millie smiles.

Portland, Plymouth, Biscay, Finisterre. Sole, Lundy, Fastnet. Most of these names are FitzRoy's. Can I make you love him?

Millie holds out her hands.

When you confessed to the absurd gesture, you became – desirable. FitzRoy was full of absurd gestures. Irish Sea, Shannon, Rockall, Malin, Hebrides, Bailey. The absurd gesture is widespread but its evolutionary purpose remains a mystery. Fair Isle, Faroes . . . unless . . . Love. Love makes you ambitious and culture uses you to multiply. My question is: could you love me?

Millie gently takes Ian's head in her hands. Then she looks up, gestures off-stage.

Millie I think it's time for you to commit suicide.

Ian and Millie leave.

SCENE SEVEN: 'EVOLUTION'

Darwin's study as it is now in Down House, some of it cordoned off. Darwin comes on, an old man, with a cane and beard, arranges some papers, eventually sits in his chair.
Millie comes on, in an outdoor jacket, carrying a bag, etc. She looks all around and then at an imaginary line of bookshelves, towards the audience.

Darwin When on board *H.M.S. Beagle*, as a naturalist, I was much struck with certain facts in the distribution of the organic beings inhabiting South America –

FitzRoy comes on, in an admiral's jacket, carrying his Bible, a bowl and a razor. Not at home, he looks around for some place to put them.

FitzRoy And the earth brought forth grass, and herb yielding seed after his kind –

Darwin – and in the geological relations of the present to the past inhabitants of the continent.

Millie (*as if reading titles*) Vestiges of the Natural History of Creation, the Meaning of Evolution . . .

Darwin These facts seem to throw some light on the origin of species –

FitzRoy – and the tree yielding fruit, whose seed was in itself after his kind – And God saw that it was good. (*He lets out a sob and closes the Bible in despair.*)

Millie Consciousness Explained . . .

Darwin – that mystery of mysteries.

Lawrence comes on, also in a jacket, with a camera. Looks around and spots Millie.

FitzRoy I left nothing behind . . .

Lawrence turns towards FitzRoy a moment.

Darwin In considering the origin of species, it is quite conceivable that a naturalist, reflecting on mutual affinities of organic beings –

Millie The Beak of the Finch, the Blind Watchmaker –

FitzRoy A light foam of ridicule and irritation, a puff of weather.

Darwin – might conclude that species had not been independently created –

FitzRoy The dark side of his light

Millie Ever since Darwin . . . The Mismeasure of Man.

Lawrence (*to Millie*) Blind kings, barren women, runaway children and castaways peopled my childhood –

FitzRoy But if you can bring me back –

Lawrence turns again to FitzRoy.

Darwin – but had descended like varieties from other species.

Millie (*still reading*) The Selfish Gene . . .

FitzRoy Give me substance –

Lawrence (*to Millie*) They became my ancestors, these loved figures carved from the crooked timber of humanity –

FitzRoy Tolerance.

Millie Life's Grandeur –

Lawrence Lining the shelves of my imagination –

Darwin From that day to the present I have steadily pursued the same object –

Lawrence Their legacy, empathy.

FitzRoy grasps Lawrence's shoulder, in the gesture of the Ancient Mariner.

FitzRoy If you can find me and give me room –

Millie (*reading*) The Language Instinct –

FitzRoy Then we become part of this, too.

Darwin My work is now nearly finished . . .

FitzRoy moves to Tom.

FitzRoy (*to Tom*) Both of us.

Tom acknowledges this, nods. FitzRoy turns towards Millie, as Lawrence hands her some notes.

All of us.

Fade.

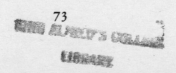